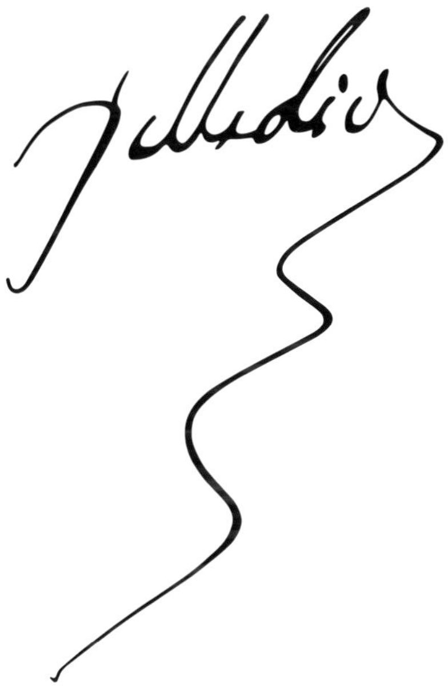

ANDREAS PALLADIVS VICENTINVS.

Paulus Caliary Veronensis effigiem pinxit.   B. Picart delineavit et sculpsit 1716.

MANFRED WUNDRAM

ANDREA PALLADIO

1508–1580

The Rules of Harmony

TASCHEN

© 2016 TASCHEN GmbH
Hohenzollernring 53, D-50672 Köln
www.taschen.com

Original edition ► © 2009 TASCHEN GmbH
Editor ► Peter Gössel, Bremen
Project management ► Swantje Schmidt, Bremen
Design and layout ► Gössel und Partner, Bremen
Text edited by ► Avinus, Berlin
Translation ► Maureen Roycroft Sommer,
  Bergisch Gladbach

Printed in Slovakia
ISBN 978–3–8365–5021–5

Illustration page 2 ► Frontispiece from *Andrea
Palladio, The Architecture of A. Palladio in Four
Books*, published by James (Giacomo) Leoni, 1715

Illustration above ► A Palace on the Water,
main façade, pencil and ink, partially coloured,
City Museum of Vicenza

Contents

6 Introduction

18 Villa Godi

22 Villa Piovene

24 Villa Forni-Cerato

26 Villa Pisani

30 Palazzo della Ragione ("Basilica")

34 Villa Poiana

36 Palazzo Chiericati

38 Villa Cornaro

42 Villa Chiericati

44 Villa Badoer

46 Villa Barbaro

52 Villa Foscari

56 Villa Emo

60 Chiesa San Giorgio Maggiore

64 Palazzo Valmarana

66 Palazzo Schio

68 Villa Almerico ("La Rotonda")

74 Villa Sarego

76 Loggia del Capitaniato

78 Chiesa del Redentore

84 Tempietto Barbaro

88 Teatro Olimpico

92 Life and Work

94 Glossary

95 Map

96 Bibliography / Credits

REGINA VIRTVS

I QVATTRO LIBRI
DELL'ARCHITETTVRA
Di Andrea Palladio.
Ne' quali, dopo un breue trattato de' cinque
ordini, & di quelli auertimenti, che sono
piu necessarij nel fabricare;
SI TRATTA DELLE CASE PRIVATE,
delle Vie, de i Ponti, delle Piazze, de i Xisti, et de' Tempij.
CON PRIVILEGI.

IN VENETIA,
Appresso Dominico de'
Franceschi.
IAC. AVG. 1570. THVANI.

Introduction

Opposite page:
Copperplate etching, title page of the 1570 edition of Andrea Palladio's *I Quattro Libri dell' Architettura*
"Regina Virtus", the "Goddess of Virtue", is seen on a throne at the top of the picture. Palladio thereby emphazises the fact that architecture must focus on general welfare.

Portal of the church Santa Maria dei Servi in Vicenza
Palladio is likely to have worked on this piece created by the workshop of Giovanni di Giacomo da Porlezza in 1531.

No other architect in the history of Western art has ever had an effect that was as spontaneous and as long lasting, indeed one that has reverberated undiminished over centuries, as did Andrea Palladio. What has come to be called Palladianism transcends the boundaries of all country-specific categories in the field of art. It not only spread to other Romanic countries, but also took hold in Germany, the Netherlands, Scandinavia and Eastern Europe, and ultimately became one of the most important roots of seventeenth and eighteenth century English architecture. And, although Palladio always focused on "pure" architecture in his creative work, the forms he established have also come to influence other areas, including English cabinet making in the nineteenth century.

Any work by an individual artist that is to find such broad emulation throughout different periods, and indeed to become a stylistic concept itself, must first have established norms and developed models that are applicable beyond the individual work. In this sense, Palladio can be seen as the first "classicist" in modern architecture, i.e. the master who, by intensively studying the architecture of classical antiquity, not only attempted to revive it for his own time, but to virtually imitate it and to establish its timeless validity. Through his own actions, Palladio made a fundamental contribution to this assessment, which resulted in a narrower focus being taken when viewing his work. He not only published *L'Antichità di Roma* as a product of his first visit to Rome in 1554, in which he takes stock of the building monuments that had been preserved or were being rediscovered in Rome in the mid-1500s, but in the introduction to his *I Quattro Libri dell'Architettura*, published in 1570, he actually states that he had chosen Vitruvius as his master and guide, since "the ancient Romans ... in building well, vastly excelled those who have been since their time." Since the architecture of Ancient Rome is undoubtedly a fundamental element in Palladio's work, the question arises as to what Palladio actually adopted from classical antiquity, and *how* he assimilated these impulses into his own artistic ideas, in relation to the task at hand and his current level of development.

Palladio was born as Andrea di Pietro, the son of a miller in Padua, on 8 November 1508. When he was thirteen, his father apprenticed him for six years to the workshop of the architect and stonemason Bartolomeo Cavazza da Sossano in Padua. To this day, little is known about the exact conditions of this apprenticeship. In April 1523 Andrea fled from Cavazza's workshop and went to Vicenza, but was forced to return and honour his contract. A year later, the young stonemason was allowed to join the Masons' and Stone Carvers' Guild in Vicenza and was hired by the respected workshop of Giovanni di Giacomo da Porlezza in Pedemuro. Initially, nothing indicated that he would become anything more than a craftsman. An attempt to establish a workshop of his own in 1530 apparently ended in failure after a short time. In 1534, Andrea was still listed as a member of the workshop in Pedemuro. The training he received seems to have been sufficient to enable Palladio to create more than just high quality objects and carvings in stone. A portal of the Church of Santa Maria dei Servi in Vicenza, which was carved by the workshop of Giovanni di Giacomo da Porlezza, is sometimes attributed to Palladio and others.

Palladio's encounter with Count Giangiorgio Trissino (1478–1550), an author of extensive writings who was highly recognized in humanist circles, is reported for 19 February 1538 in Vicenza. We have no information concerning the personal relationship between the young stonemason, who was allowed to assume the title of architect on 26 August 1540, and the Vicentine nobleman. However, Trissino seems to have aided Andrea di Pietro in gaining access to an exclusive circle of clients in Vicenza and made it possible for him to undertake an extensive study of contemporary and Roman architecture. In summer 1541 he embarked, presumably in the company of his patron, on a first journey to Rome; it was followed by a second, longer journey undertaken together from the late autumn of 1545 into the first months of 1546. Trissino was also responsible for bestowing the name "Palladio" upon the architect in 1545, after Pallas Athena, the goddess of the arts. During another journey to Rome in 1546–1547, Palladio also devoted himself to studies in Tivoli, Palestrina and Albano. His hope of being appointed to the building lodge of Saint Peter's in Rome was dashed by Pope Paul III's death. Palladio published *L'Antichità di Roma* in 1554 as the fruit of his journey to Rome.

The first evidence of Palladio's activities as an architect is from the 1540s. After constructing a series of villas around Vicenza and his impressive commission for the Palazzo Thiene in Vicenza, a first highpoint in his career followed with his designation, on 11 April 1549, as chief architect of the so-called Basilica, the loggia for the Palazzo della Ragione in Vicenza. Palladio can be seen from that point on as one of the most important master builders in Northern Italy, alongside the older Jacopo Sansovino (1486–1570) und Michele Sanmicheli (1484–1559), both of whom he was soon to eclipse in terms of his importance for the development of architecture. Palladio's fame soon spread. Around 1550 he struck up a friendship with the Venetian patrician Daniele Barbaro, who introduced him to aristocratic circles in Venice. A journey to Trento in 1552 at the invitation of Prince-Bishop Cardinal Christoforo Madruzzi, on whose initiative the Council of Trent was convened in 1545, was augmented by a stay in Innsbruck.

By no means an early developer, Palladio reached the pinnacle of his intellectual and professional development at the beginning of the fifth decade of his life. Well-trained as a craftsman, familiar with architectural history and with a broad range of humanistic interests, he was able to pursue his fantasy in all directions. In the 1550s he completed a series of impressive villas for aristocrats in Vicenza and in Venice.

Villa architecture was, however, only one of the focal points of Palladio's work. Beginning in the 1560s, imposing palaces and palace façades began to play a larger role, particularly in Vicenza, while in Venice, where the "painterly" palace façades were to remain foreign to Palladio's "classical style", ecclesiastical architecture offered him an opportunity to realize impressive projects: after the cloister of Santa Maria della Carità in 1560–1561, the refectory of the monastery of San Giorgio Maggiore in 1560–1562, and his design for the façade of San Francesco della Vigna in 1562, the cornerstone was laid for the church of San Giorgio Maggiore in 1565, and the construction of the pilgrimage church Il Redentore began in 1576—works that are just as important in terms of architectural history as are his secular buildings.

Palladio's prestige among his contemporaries grew continually. In 1556, he was one of the founding members of the "Olympian Academy" in Vicenza. In 1566, he travelled to Turin as a guest of Duke Emanuele Filiberto of Savoy and travelled on to Provence

Portrait of Giangiorgio Trissino, by Vincenzo di Biagio (called: Catena), executed between 1525 and 1527
Louvre, Paris

Andrea Palladio, study of a capital
This study may have been based on sketches that Palladio completed during his trip to Rome in 1545–1547.

from there. That same year, the Accademia del Disegno in Florence inducted him as a member. In 1568, he was forced to decline an invitation to the Imperial court in Vienna because he had too much work. In 1570, he followed in Sansovino's footsteps as the advising architect in Venice.

During the final decades of his career, the artistic solutions and modes of expression he employed became more richly diverse. Palladio did not simply vary his buildings by drawing from an established repertoire of details and compositions, he explored new areas of artistic design as he progressed from one major work to the next. In doing so he always took the geographic conditions or the urban context in which the building was to be erected into consideration, especially with regard to its visibility and function. His reputation seems to have allowed him to take unusual liberties in dealing with his clients.

In the last year of his life, he was finally able to fulfil two ambitions that he had long entertained both in his thoughts and designs: the Olympic Society in Vicenza commissioned him with the planning of the Teatro Olympico and his old Venetian friend and patron, Marcantonio Barbaro, commissioned him with the construction of a family chapel near the Villa Barbaro in Maser in the form of a central plan church. Palladio died on 19 August 1580 while these buildings were still under construction, either in Vicenza or while overseeing the work on the Tempietto in Maser.

We know very little about Palladio's personality—surprisingly little for an age in which artists' biographies and anecdotes about artists were ever more frequently recorded. Information about his family is only found in lifeless documents: one of these is an assessment of the dowry provided for his wife, Allegradona, by her carpenter father, dated 14 April 1534. We also know that this marriage produced four sons— Leonida, Marcantonio, Orazio and Silla—as well as one daughter, Zenobia. The death of two sons, Leonida and Orazio, in short succession in early 1572, was a deep blow to the father.

In his dealings with clients and with workers Palladio seems to have been friendly, attentive and charming. Contemporaries report that he provided the members of his own workshop with the same thorough training that he had received in the Pedemuro workshop, and could instil a sense of joy in anyone at completing assigned tasks.

Attempts to find the key to Palladio's works in his character and biography are destined to fail because his works reveal not even the slightest detail concerning his personality. Hence the danger of drawing false conclusions from the reciprocal interpretation of artistic phenomena and personal temperament, which so often caused outstanding artists of the sixteenth century to be misunderstood, can be precluded.

Through his own remarks, Palladio channelled all attempts at interpretation towards classical antiquity—or at least suggested that the standards of antiquity were the only ones that should be applied in judging his works. But no master is able to develop in complete independence of the artistic context within which he comes of age. Accordingly, the roots from which Palladio derived his style can be found within the context of the architecture that was contemporary or relatively recent in his time. In his early villas, such as the Villa Godi in Lugo di Vicenza, Palladio not only continued to build the type of two-tower villa characteristic of the Veneto, he also drew upon the ideals that had served the generation of his teachers in using a rhythmic order of closed surfaces and openings. The sculptural articulation of the wall became less important than the dominating surface.

Giulio Romano, Palazzo del Te in Mantua, 1525–1535
Portico to the garden

In the following years, Palladio reversed the relationship between the wings and principle block of the building; it is no longer the wings that project forward (as *risalito*), but instead the central axis, which is also emphasized by a gable. In this context, one finds the principle block opening either in a so-called *serliana* motif (Villa Forni-Cerato in Montecchio Precalcino) or in three uniform arches (Villa Gazzotti-Grimani in Bertesina). For the first time, an emphasis on the volume and centring is manifested. Palladio chose a two-storey portico as a means of emphasizing the principle block for the first time in 1552, for the Villa Pisani in Montagnana and, one year later, for the Villa Cornaro in Piombino Dese, and he used a colossal order under a gable, a "temple front", as the predominant motif for the Villa Chiericati in Vancimuglio in 1554. The influence of the studies he undertook in Rome can be easily recognized in the whole as well as in the formulation of the details.

Attempts to determine an invariable constant in Palladio's work, or an unwavering direction in his development, are doomed to failure. First of all, Palladio's artistic temperament was too agile not to be continually absorbing and synthesizing new impressions, and, secondly, he always reacted in a very sensitive manner to the requirements of the client, the building's function and its location.

Around 1542, Palladio received what seems to have been his first commission to build a city palace, the Palazzo Thiene in Vicenza. Even in this early phase, Palladio demonstrated his ability to make allowances for what the clients needed and wanted. There is no overlooking the fact that he also engaged in a dialogue with contemporary architecture here. His sympathy for the canon of forms developed by Giulio Romana is particularly obvious. Yet he did not simply use his motifs—for example windows framed by corbels—he put them at the service of his own architectural statements, for example by framing the columns with the corbels.

With his loggia for the Palazzo della Ragione in Vicenza, the so-called Basilica, Palladio reached one of the first pinnacles of his career. Of all of Palladio's works, the Basilica, along with the Villa Rotonda and the Il Redentore church, is one of the most frequently emulated, and it also set the standard for Palladio's relationship to Roman antiquity. The use of individual classical details requires no explanation.

Window of the Palazzo Thiene in Vicenza, 1542–1558, framed by corbels
The design for the palace, which was never completed, is attributed to Giulio Romano, Palladio assumed responsibility for planning the construction and, after Romano's death in 1546, for overseeing construction as well.

Right:
The completed façades of the Palazzo Thiene; originally planned to be much larger, they face onto narrow side streets.

Did the model character of antiquity, often cited by Palladio, mean more to him than simply using individual details adopted from classical Roman architecture? It inspired the symmetry inherent in each of Palladio's works, regardless of the adoption of single formal elements—a symmetry that had led Vitruvius, whom he much admired, to say: that in every good building there must be a harmonious relationship between the individual elements of the work and between the different parts and the whole. Palladio's affinity for antiquity was based on this fundamental principle.

However, Palladio cites a second decisive referential context in his own writings for understanding his work. In *I Quattro libri dell'Architettura* he makes a statement that has been almost entirely ignored by the research: "I say therefore, that architecture, as well as all other arts, being an *imitatrix* of nature can suffer nothing that either alienates or deviates from that which is agreeable to nature".

As understood in his time, nature was not the antithesis of the technical-industrial world, but rather a concept that helped to explain how everything around us, from animals to the planets, functioned. The inalienable laws of nature derived by man from its economic principles and the aesthetic principles it exhibited applied analogously to

architecture. Accordingly, people not only believed that there was one objectively correct design, which reflected a form of divine intervention, but also that it was necessary to create a harmony in all works defined not only by the uniform design of the building itself, but also by its integration into the landscape or urban context.

Palladio never intended his works to be seen as artefacts clearly distinguished from nature or the landscape, but as entering into union with it. Many of his major works are best understood from this perspective: the hilly location of the Villa Rotonda, the consideration of canal frontage in situating the Villa Foscari in Malcontenta, just beyond the gates to Venice, the expansive character of the Villa Barbaro in Maser set against a low range of hills, the opening of the main façade, unusual for his city palaces, in the Palazzo Chiericati, when it faced what was then the harbour of Vicenza, the extraordinarily pronounced sculptural articulation of the façade of S. Giorgio Maggiore in Venice, which commandingly draws all eyes to it from the Piazzetta di San Marco where the Canale della Giudecca and the Canale Grande flow into Saint Mark's Basin. Palladio's genius was, to a great extent, based on this sensitive reaction to the surrounding context in combination with elements of classical Roman architecture, it therefore defies imitation that is limited to the buildings' formal appearance.

In the case of the Palazzo Iseppo Porto, focus is again on classical antiquity. In this project, which was presumably begun around 1549/50, Palladio attempted to revive the classical organization of internal rooms—in his treatise he specifically cites the Greek tradition. This relates both to the concept of the peristyle court as well as to the strict separation of the owner's living quarters from those of the guests.

The façade of the Palazzo Iseppo Porto, by contrast, was born of a design concept of Palladio's own time. The lower level and the *piano nobile* are clearly separated from each other: the rusticated blocks on the lower level also help to illustrate this separation, one that corresponds with the difference in the importance of the two floors.

Façade of the Palazzo Iseppo Porto in Vicenza
From *I Quattro Libri dell'Architettura*, 1570, volume 2, page 9

In the works of his mature and late periods, however, Palladio turned to the idea of drawing the façade together through uninterrupted vertical articulation, and began to overcome the specifically manneristic fragmentation of wall surfaces to the benefit of greater unity. The fact that Palladio adopted and developed the idea of drawing façades together through uninterrupted vertical articulation as a matter of principle, is demonstrated by works from his mature and late period; the Villa Barbaro in Maser, for which he drew up the plans in 1557/58, accentuates the principle block by using a colossal order which can be seen in the frontal view. Other examples are the façade of the Church of San Giorgio Maggiore in Venice, the Palazzo Valmarana in Vicenza, planned in 1565, and in a number of variations in his late works, such as the Loggia del Capitaniato and the Palazzo Porto Breganze in Vicenza, the Villa Sarego in Pedemonte di Valpolicella and the façade of the Il Redentore church in Venice.

In 1560 Palladio succeeded in gaining a foothold in Venice for the first time in conjunction with the construction of monasteries and churches. After completing the cloisters of Santa Maria dell Carità (1560–1569) and the refectory of San Giorgio Maggiore (1560–1562), as well as the design of the façade of San Francesco della Vigna (after 1562), he was commissioned to build a Benedictine monastery church, San Giorgio Maggiore, in 1565, and in 1576/77 his activities in the field of ecclesiastical architecture were crowned by his plans for the votive church Il Redentore. The fact that Palladio, whose architectural ideas stood in stark contrast to the Venetian tradition, was ultimately entrusted with such prominent projects in the heart of the Republic was not only

a result of his friendly relationship with the Venetian patricians. There was, in fact, no other serious competitor, in either artistic or technical terms, in all of Northern Italy after the mid-sixteenth century. The traditional plan for a domed cruciform church had been further refined in buildings like San Salvatore in Venice (1507–1534, presumably according to plans drawn up by Tullio Lombardi in consultation with Jacopo Sansovino) and Santa Giustina in Padua (begun by Andrea Moroni in 1532). By the time new construction was begun on the Church of San Giuliano in Venice in 1553, Jacopo Sansovino, who was the Republic's advising architect, was no longer able to contribute innovative ideas: it was built as a simple hall church with three chapels around the presbytery. Palladio seems to have been chosen not only because of his well-established reputation, but also because of the unusual requirements: as had been the case with San Giorgio Maggiore, considerations related to the urban context played an important role in connection with Il Redentore. Both façades were expected to establish a visual connection to the Piazzetta di San Marco across Saint Mark's Basin, in the one case, and the Canale di Giudecca, in the other. No other architect at this time seemed as predestined for this task as Palladio, who was known for considering the situation of a building in the landscape or the urban context, and for taking views of the building from both distant and varying standpoints into consideration.

Palladio executed his tasks with aplomb. Although the two major churches are of fundamentally different types—San Giorgio Maggiore is a three-nave, cruciform basilica, the Redentore a longitudinal nave with a centralizing eastern end—in terms of the intention of their designs they are closely related. In both cases Palladio was striving to create a unified space flooded with light. In each case the walls appear to be the sum of highly sculptured individual elements, and in both buildings Palladio was striving to integrate the longitudinal nave and the central plan. In this respect, when compared to San Giorgio Maggiore, Il Redentore is—the more highly differentiated form.

Despite the highly diverse conditions, in terms of location, function and the material resources of his clients, the question still arises as to both the artistic constant and stylistic development of Palladio's works. The constant has already been cited: it can be found in the unerring sense of proportion, symmetry and order that connects Palladio with antiquity and which he admired in antiquity. At the same time, there is no over-looking the astonishingly broad spectrum of development between his early works and his late period. In essence, Palladio can be seen to have been striving for a higher de-gree of unity from one decade to the next. While the whole initially seems like the sum of its parts, i.e. like a form of "addition", Palladio increasingly developed the idea of a whole, in which the details are assigned an inalienable place. In his façades and court-yards, and not least of all in his church buildings, Palladio attained this unity mainly by drawing the buildings together along vertical lines, while in his floor plans he tended to rely on the formation of a centre around which subsidiary rooms were symmetrically grouped, although economic constraints often prohibited the execution of such ideas. Concurrently, Palladio further reduced the decorative elements, which he had always used only sparingly, in order not to compromise the appearance of pure architecture. In those cases in Palladio's late work where there was lavish decoration—as is the case with the façades of the Pallazo Barbarano or the Loggia del Capitaniato—it was only applied after the fact, added to the existing surface, and never developed out of the structure of the building.

Ultimately, during the four decades in which we are able to follow the development of Palladio's work, we can see an increasing tendency to sculpturally form façades and interior spaces, which led, in his late work, almost to the point of a surging and re-ceding modulation of surfaces. In this respect, Andrea Palladio was as important in illustrating perspectives for the future as Michelangelo was in his work on Saint Peter's in Rome.

Along with questions as to the constants and the variables in Palladio's work, one is simultaneously confronted with the problem of its stylistic classification. As a "clas-sicist", whose primary orientation is considered to have been towards the architecture of antiquity, the most likely characterization would be as an heir to the High Renais-sance period. He did indeed continue to develop certain elements of the High Renais-sance. One indication is his renewed interest in the idea of a "pure" central plan, which he was ultimately able to realize twice—in the Villa Rotonda and in the Tempietto at the Villa Barbaro. The organization of the interior space in his two major churches around the dominant element of the dome can also be seen as a legacy of the High Renais-sance and a reflection of his admiration for Michelangelo, in as much as we can classify his work as what Heinrich Wölfflin described as the "Classic Art" of the stylistic periods after Antiquity. Ultimately, it is the harmony of the individual parts, which are visibly related to each other as well as to the whole, that makes Palladio's work seem as if it should not be classified as belonging to his own age, which is now generally re-ferred to as "Mannerism".

On the other hand, Palladio, as a phenomenon, illustrates just how difficult it is to get a firm grasp on the ambiguous concept of "Mannerism". Although the roots of Palladio's work can be traced back to the High Renaissance, in many details it even proves to be anti-classic in a sixteenth century sense. A careful examination of his works makes this clear in a number of ways: for example his tendency to create space within walls by suspending the simple division between the exterior and interior with

different layers, and thus establishing public space within a building, as he did in the Basilica in Vicenza, can neither be explained by precedents established in Classical Antiquity nor in the High Renaissance. The realization of "ideal" central plan architecture and the simultaneous reversal of this concept—namely by initially concentrating space at the centre and then employing only centrifugal forces with an outward thrust—as found in the Villa Rotondo, can be seen as a basic principle of Mannerist art: the interpretation of a "classic" model with non-classical means. In a similar manner, the Villa Rotonda offers the synthesis of another contradiction: the model of a perfectly symmetrical cube, both in its external and internal design, with four six-columned porticoes, a somewhat abstract concept that blends in with the topography of the surrounding countryside in an unparalleled manner: elements of the abstract and concrete, rational and emotional all intersect. Moreover, the series of the columns that separates the presbytery from the monk's choir in San Giorgio Maggiore and as well as in Il Redentore allow a view from the longitudinal nave into a distance that cannot be gauged by the eye—the actual and the optical elongation diverge, and attention is cautiously drawn here to the seemingly endless depths of perspective in paintings from that period, e.g. in the work of Jacopo Tintoretto.

The list of observations that can be cited to prove that Palladio was indeed a "Mannerist" could be easily extended. At the same time, the inadequacy of categorization in stylistic periods that are necessarily based on generalizations must also be considered, since the suspension of clearly defined spatial boundaries and the divergence of the actual and visual scale of space are also basic characteristics of the Baroque period. The tendency to draw the architecture together by employing vertical lines of sight and the evolution from the emphasis on surfaces towards the dominance of sculptural elements also speak for Baroque architecture. In this sense, Palladio, who was undoubtedly the most important European architect between Michelangelo, on the one hand, and Bernini and Borromini, on the other, can be described as a decisive pioneer of Baroque. Regardless of how great Vignola's contribution to the development of Baroque ecclesiastical architecture was, by introducing the detailed division of both façade and interior wall surfaces in constructing the Il Gésu church in Rome as of 1568 as well as in terms of the clear determination of spatial boundaries, he was far more obliged to the Late Renaissance than Palladio was in Il Redentore.

Individual works by Palladio have found quite obvious emulation, both in the form of direct copies and variations. Palladio's determining influence on the "style classique", i.e. French and English Baroque, and on late eighteenth and early nineteenth century Classicism is unique.

Opposite page:
Il Redentore in Venice, 1576–1592

1537 ▸ Villa Godi
Via Palladio, Lugo di Vicenza

This well preserved building is considered one of Palladio's earliest works. It was completed, presumably in around 1540, before Palladio's first trip to Rome. Although he had already been inspired to study antiquity through his relationship to Giangiorgio Trissino, this building shows Palladio still trying to come to terms with the architecture of his own time. The form of the Villa Godi seems to echo that of the villa of his patron, Trissino, in Cricoli, on which Palladio had worked while still an architect in the Pedemuro workshop. In both buildings a recessed principle block is flanked by two projecting wings. Both buildings are also axially symmetric. However, the fact that the villas are independent of each other is demonstrated by Palladio's altogether different approach to the two-tower villa so typical of the Veneto: the middle part of the villa seems to be ensconced between the massive projecting wings (risalites), which are each considerably wider than the principle block. The relationship between the wing and the principle block usually found in two-tower villas is thereby completely reversed. In this context, the wings play a far more important role in visual terms than the principle block does. Although the entire garden front is articulated by rhythmically recurrent vertical axes, a visual counterpoint to the central axis of the façade as a whole is established by the groups of double windows on the façades of the wings. The voids created by this articulation of the wing façades allow these smooth, untreated wall areas to determine the appearance of the façade in such a way that they make the wings seem far more massive than any element of the principle block of the building. On the contrary, the *piano nobile* is opened up by a loggia backed by a triple arch; in the lower storey two

arcades, which are visually introduced by two blind arches on the lower storey of the wings, flank the stairway that leads to the loggia. Up above, the final features are two so-called mezzanine or half-storey windows between which the crest of the Godi family is embedded in the masonry. The impression from the other sides of the villa is quite different; while the primary block is recessed in the front, it projects on the park side from the remainder of the building's volume. Palladio must have seen the building's volume as a clearly defined block, from which nothing could be subtracted without it being added somewhere else. The *serliana* on this back façade was not part of the original plan: it replaced a thermal window in 1550, whilst Palladio was called in to do renovations when frescoes were being painted in the main hall of the *piano nobile*.

The Hall of the Muses with frescoes by Battista del Moro

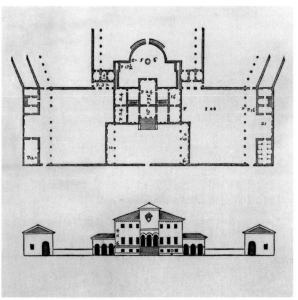

The salon with scenes symbolizing peace and justice
A common theme following the War of the League of Cambrai

Left:
Plan and courtyard façade
From *I Quattro Libri dell'Architettura*, 1570, volume 2, page 65

1539 ▸ Villa Piovene
Via Palladio, Lugo di Vicenza

View of the façade

The Villa Piovene was, as seems to be indicated by existing documents, originally smaller than it presents itself today. The loggia which projects from the centre—six slender Ionic columns supporting a triangular gable—was begun by Palladio in 1540 and only completed after his death in 1587. The main house seems to have been expanded through the addition of the vertical window axis on either side in the 1570s; they were executed in Palladio's spirit, although not by him. The double staircase, which leads from the lower floor to the loggia, and the two *barchessas* are attributed to Francesco Muttoni. Although Palladio's authorship has not been accepted without controversy, and cannot be assumed for the entire ensemble, the main house does seem to have been based on his design and executed in his spirit, at least in terms of the formulation of the façade.

View from the front loggia

Just as in the case of the Villa Godi, the façade of the Villa Piovene was designed to leave large areas of smooth, unmodulated wall surface, the serenity of which was considerably compromised by later additions, whereas the original design with three arches in the principle block of the *piano nobile* and a simple stairway leading up to them would have emphasized serenity.

1541▸Villa Forni-Cerato
Via Venezia, Montecchio Precalcino, Vicenza

Opposite page:
Garden façade

Right:
Cross-section drawing by Ottavio Bertotti Scamozzi
From Ottavio Bertotti Scamozzi, *Le fabbriche e i disegni di Andrea Palladio*, 1796, volume 2, plate 35

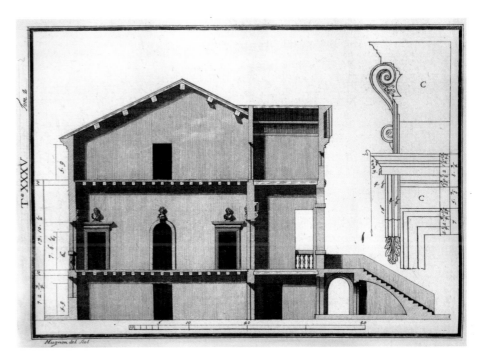

Below:
Façade reliefs
The depictions of river gods are copies of originals by Alessandro Vittoria.

Palladio was first cited as the architect in charge of building this villa by Francesco Muttoni and Ottavio Bertotti Scamozzi in the eighteenth century. Today, nearly all researchers agree with the opinion of these two architects. The villa itself also provides further evidence of who was responsible for its creation between 1541 and 1542.

In terms of length and width, the building is relatively small; its height is divided into three elements: a cellar, *piano nobile* and a mezzanine. Its width is also determined by three elements. The loggia projects from the façade as the most dominant. In remarkable similarity to the Villa Godi, a stairway, the height of the cellar level, leads up to the loggia, which opens in a *serliana*. This takes up the entire width of the loggia and lends it unusual visual emphasis.

The Villa Forni-Cerato provides the first example of the subjugation of the individual details of a façade in relation to the entire façade that was to become characteristic of Palladio's later development.

1542 ▸ Villa Pisani

Via Risaie, Bagnolo di Lonigo, Vicenza

The main residence is all that remains of the *villa rustica* that the Pisanis had built in 1542. Its façade overlooks the navigable Guà River; hence it has a public character. Here again Palladio made use of the traditional two-tower façade, although the towers are only slightly taller than the mass of the cubic building. The dominant element is a loggia, which has three arches and is complemented by a triangular gable over a triglyph frieze. The arcature is artfully designed: an exciting play of light and shadow results from the rustication of the six Tuscan order pilasters—two on either end and one between each of the openings. However, this rustication was only worked into the mortar, since the reveals were not plastered.

A view of the courtyard façade reveals the fenestration so typical of Palladio in these years. The central axis is emphasized by the thermal window. The effect that this window actually has would have been even more pronounced if the planned porch supported by four columns had also been built. The Pisanis received their guests in the large hall with a cruciform floor plan and ceiling frescoes by an unknown sixteenth century artist. According to the original plan, the thermal window on the garden façade was to have a counterpart on the river side. However, the massive gable precluded the execution of

Above:
Façade facing the River Guà

Left:
Courtyard façade
As the wings of the building no longer exist, the villa now stands all alone in the greenery of the garden.

Plan and elevation

From *I Quattro Libri dell' Architettura*, 1570, volume 2, page 47

Below:
Palladio's sketch of the plan

Bottom:
Palladio's design for the courtyard façade and plan of the building

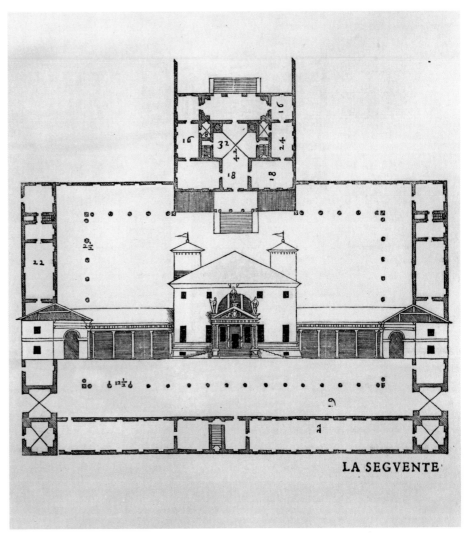

LA SEGVENTE·

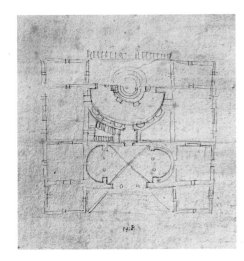

this solution. An assessment of the property dating from 1544 indicates that the villa was habitable at this time, at least the main residence seems to have already been completed. Around 1560 Palladio again became involved with the Villa Pisani when the agricultural wings were built.

1546 ▸ Palazzo della Ragione ("Basilica")
Loggia ▸ Piazza dei Signori, Vicenza

Opposite page:
View through the loggia on the lower level

Drawing of the two right yokes
From *I Quattro Libri dell'Architettura*, 1570,
volume 3, page 43

Right:
***The Feast in the House of Levi* by Paolo
Veronese, 1573**
Galleria dell'Accademia, Venice

With the so-called Basilica, which is in fact the double-storey loggia, that was built around the older Palazzo Pubblico or Palazzo della Ragione (i.e. city hall), Palladio established his reputation.

In 1458, work on the new Palazzo della Ragione was completed. The master builder in charge was presumably Domenico da Venezia. The lower level consisted of a columned hall, and the upper storey was a single large hall (or *sala*). The notion of building a series of arcades on the side facing the Piazza dei Signori was entertained for the first time roughly two decades later. After a long interruption, plans were finally drawn up for the construction of an ensemble for the city hall in Vicenza modelled on the arcades of the Palazzo della Ragione in Padua, which were built between 1420 and 1435. After a complicated planning process, which involved most of the notable architects in Northern Italy, Palladio was commissioned with the execution of the building on 11 April 1549. The fact that Palladio had the arcades in Padua in mind is demonstrated by the motifs he borrowed: the circular openings (*oculi*) in the spandrels of the arches, that made an important contribution to the spatialization of the wall in Vicenza, were adopted from Padua. Otherwise, it is hard to imagine how the differences between the two buildings could have been any greater: while in Padua the broader arches on the lower level correspond with two openings on the upper level supported by delicate marble columns, in Vicenza the openings in the arcade are identical in size and shape on both the upper and lower levels. Instead of a long series of round arches, Palladio uses the so-called *serliana* motif, a combination similar to a triumphal arch with a wide arch in the middle flanked by two openings, i.e. rectangular openings, enclosed at the top by an architrave. Palladio may have been inspired to connect the inside and outside in this manner by the garden loggia designed by Giulio Romano for the Palazzo del Te, which was built between 1524 and 1526.

Palladio did not employ this motif in the traditional form, instead he extended it into a third dimension, here again further developing an idea borrowed from Giulio

Elevation and plan
From I *Quattro Libri dell'Architettura*, 1570, volume 3, page 42

Romano, who used this motif to emphasize the middle arch of the garden loggia of the Palazzo del Te. The columns of the *serliana* are doubled towards the interior of the loggia. This makes the round archway into a sort of shallow barrel vault; small nearly rectangular yokes are created between the double columns and between the delimiting pilasters. A great deal of spatialization characterizes the wall. This is where the real "Palladio motif" was created, one that was destined to find surprisingly broad proliferation in the following period. It can be found on the upper level of the cloisters of the Convento do Cristo in Tomar (Portugal), begun by Diego de Torralva in 1566 and completed by Filippo Terzi around 1580, as well as in the model for a hall on Perlachplatz in Augsburg created by Joseph Heintz in 1609. It even transcended the boundaries of artistic disciplines: in Veronese's painting *The Feast in the House of Levi* (1573) in the Galleria dell'Accademia in Venice it appears as a free-standing architectural element in the foreground.

The fact that Palladio succeeded—despite what seems to be a rigorous tendency towards unification—to create extremely vital architecture through an inexhaustibly

View of the long northern façade facing the Piazza dei Signori

rich variation of details, was one of the essential factors in determining the meaning of his work.

The work dragged on, progressing slowly due to delays caused by financial crises. On 23 July 1561, the nine arcades on the ground floor facing the Piazza dei Signori, the four adjacent ones on the narrow western side, and the only one foreseen for the east side were finally completed. The decision to build the upper loggia was not made until 6 March 1564. Palladio did not live to see the building completed. The last payment was recorded on 14 March 1617. The sculptural decoration was not completed until the middle of the seventeenth century.

Palladio is responsible for the structure's generally being referred to as the "Basilica", since in his estimation the functions of a "modern" Palazzo della Ragione (Palazzo Pubblico) were similar to those of the market basilica of antiquity—a market, an exchange and a court of law.

1548 ▸ Villa Poiana
Via Castello, Poiana Maggiore, Vicenza

Opposite page:
The fresco by Anselmo Canera, depicts an ancient sacrificial rite (around 1550).

Right:
The main façade

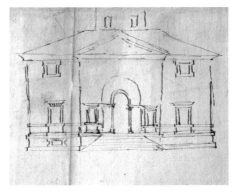

Palladio's sketch of the façade

Between 1548 and 1549 Bonifacio Poiana commissioned Andrea Palladio to build a country house. The solution that Palladio presented is considered one of his most beautiful buildings. Located on a hill, the Villa Poiana attracts attention by virtue of its simple form. Its proportions are well balanced: the individual segments of the two main façades stand in a 1:2:1 relationship to each other. The most prominent element is the primary block, the façade of which projects and has narrow bands of moulding continuing on around the corners. A motif can be found on this projecting block with which Palladio had already experimented in the elevation sketches of some of his early villa designs: the interrupted gable. The interruption of the corbelled cornice allows it to blend in organically with the wall surface of the projecting central block. A simple *serliana* provides a central focus on both the front and the back façades. Palladio presents this motif here in a notable variation, allowing it to extend into a doubled arch that frames five *oculi* between the extrados of the smaller and the intrados of the larger. Supported by the two windows on the sides of the *serliana*, it stands in a direct relationship to the projecting gable and dispels the classic portico motif, consisting of an arch, an architrave and a gable, in favour of an organic blending of elements.

The Villa Poiana displays no decorative elements. The *serliana* looks almost like it was cut into the masonry, and it is supported by simple, smoothly plastered columns. The window sills display only a slight return and merge with the continuing cornice. Only the cornices over the windows project appreciably from the masonry. The lack of decorative elements is related to the military tradition of the Poiana and reflects a building tradition that expresses a defensive stance by avoiding all forms of *decoro*.

1550 ‣ Palazzo Chiericati
Piazza Matteotti, Vicenza

View through the loggia on the lower level

Opposite page:
Main façade

Right:
Façade sketch by Palladio's son Orazio

The Palazzo Chiericati, which was begun in 1551, is the only palace built by Palladio that opens onto a piazza. The fact that the architecture, which is located near the former harbour, is open across the entire breadth seems to support the assumption that the Palazzo is a kind of "villa marittima", a villa located near the sea. It may have been planned as part of an ensemble grouped around a piazza, which Palladio was designing according to models from ancient Rome.

There is a surprising contrast, in artistic terms, to the loggia of the Palazzo della Ragione (the "Basilica"), which was under construction on the Piazza dei Signori at the same time. The eleven axes are rhythmically articulated on both levels with three axes on either side of the five central axes that project from the front of the building and a doubling of the columns at either end. In contrast to the artful interpenetration of horizontal and vertical elements characteristic of the loggia of the Palazzo della Ragione, the resting layers are a dominant theme in the Palazzo Chiericati. A massive Doric cornice made of simple metopes and triglyphs marks the separation between the two storeys, and is augmented by the sequences of balusters between the columns of the upper storey. The upper storey is topped off by a uniform, gradually staggered cornice. The sculptures that emphasize the vertical lines were only added later. The execution of the *piano nobile* diverges from Palladio's original design. According to his design, the five middle axes of the upper storey would have been open, which would have made the sequence of intervals on both floors perfectly symmetrical. However, the client wanted a larger hall (*sala*) for festivities, and by annexing this part of the loggia, the space could be doubled.

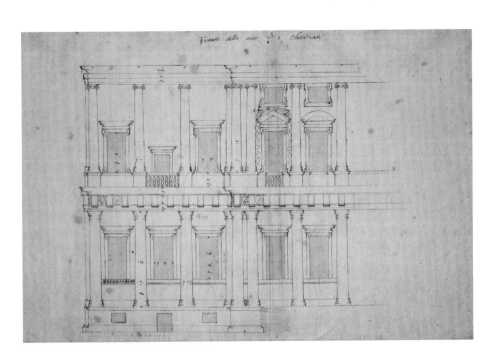

1553 · Villa Cornaro
Via Roma, Piombino Dese, Padua

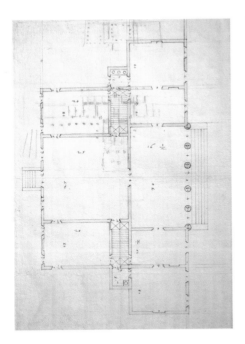

Plan sketched by Andrea Palladio

Opposite page:
Garden façade

The Villa Cornaro is much like the villa that Andrea Palladio was building for Francesco Pisani in Montagnana at roughly the same time. In 1553, the primary block seems to have already been completed. Its final completion took until sometime in the seventeenth century.

Palladio's earlier villas were characterized by floor plans oriented to the width of the building. Because the locations of the rooms in the villas were also reflected in the façades, this led to a clear separation of residential and public functions.

The intention of harmoniously combining residential and representative functions was demonstrated for the first time in the Villa Poiana. These efforts are clearly continued in the Villa Cornaro. In contrast to the earlier villas, the floor plan of the main house here is nearly perfectly square. Corresponding to the building itself, the *sala* also has a square floor plan. By virtue of its size, it serves as an intermediary between the entrance hall and the recessed garden loggia. In this context, it is remarkable that the wings of the building are harmoniously integrated into the disposition of the rooms. They are identical in width with the two rooms to either side of the entrance hall. This organic combination of the more prestigious areas with the functional ones is new, as is the central location of the large *sala*.

The Villa Cornaro differs from buildings of the *villa rustica* type, which are characteristically one-storey ensembles, as a result of the doubling of the *piano nobile*, hence it is more similar to a *villa suburbana*, a country house located just beyond the gates of the city. This typological relationship is also expressed in other respects: although a little river flows by the side of the villa, its main façade is oriented towards the street that leads past the villa. The doubling of the *piano nobile* corresponds with the construction of two loggias, one above the other. Both the garden loggia and the loggia of the main façade are supported by free-standing columns. The recessed loggia on the garden façade allows the columns to stand free; while the columns on the main façade, by contrast, are set in front of the building block like a porch. The inner disposition of the villa can also be recognized by the external design.

The organic combination of functional and residential areas is also reflected in the façade. The Ionic entablature of the order used in the lower storey rests like a belt around the two wings and the main residence. Nevertheless, the subordinate position of the wings is still expressed. The second storey is not continued to the wings. Instead of a second storey, the wings have mezzanine levels, which are noticeably lower than the second storey of the main house.

Above:
Garden façade

Left:
The lower loggia overlooking the garden

Opposite page:
Hall with four columns
The first heir to the villa had six sculptures created by Camillo Mariani, sometime after 1588, installed in the main hall. The niches were already included in Palladio's plan. The statues represent the first ancestral gallery featuring life-size figures in the history of Renaissance sculpture.

1555 ▸ Villa Chiericati
Via Nazionale, Vancimuglio, Vicenza

Opposite page:
Façade

Right:
View from the main gate

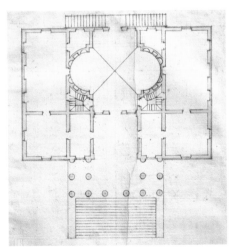

Plan sketched by Andrea Palladio

The attribution of this villa to Palladio cannot be made with absolute certainty. We know more about the time at which the villa was built than about the builder. In his will, dated 29 April 1557, Giovanni Chiericati requested that his heirs complete the building that was already under construction. Presumably the villa was close to completion at that time; the designs were presumably drawn up between 1550 and 1554.

A decisive factor in attributing the building to Palladio is its stylistic characteristics; here we find a number of elements that are closely related to other works by Palladio, alongside noticeable differences in relation to his previous villas. In front of the cubic block formed by the main building, the columned front that projects only on one side of this façade forms a rectangular block of its own with walls on the sides that are more closed than in Piombino Dese. The colossal order instead of the two storeys can be seen to anticipate the Villas Malcontenta and La Rotonda.

While the façade is strongly focused on the middle, on the one hand, the window axes, which have been shifted to the far edge of the wall, introduce more centripetal accents—a preliminary example of the sort of tension that would characterize the Villa Rotonda, albeit in a much differentiated form?

Also notable are the unusual expanses of unarticulated wall surface between the rectangular windows and the mezzanine: where one would usually expect to find the *piano nobile*, there are closed wall surfaces. The articulation of the flanks in the same tact—four window axes, i.e. no emphasis on the middle—is also unusual for Palladio.

1556 ▸ Villa Badoer
Via Giovanni Tasso, Fratta Polesine, Rovigo

View into the *barchessas*

This villa is characterized as an agricultural building by its one storey elevation and the expansive barchessas, the covered arcades on either side of the main house. The ensemble, which has been preserved in unusually good condition, must have been built around 1556. The only structures that are not part of the original are the functional wings. During the eighteenth century they were expanded and extended all the way to the front walls of the estate. Before that, they terminated at the same point as the barchessas. The entire estate is remarkably homogeneous. When studies of villas in the Veneto describe the way the *barchessas* open up to the front, they often compare them to human arms. This comparison is particularly valid in the case of the Villa Badoer. The functional wings here are, as is the case with many other villas, at a right angle to the main house; but this is downplayed by the layout of the barchessas in a quarter-circle, which inevitably catch visitors' eyes and directs their attention towards the main house, which is raised up above ground level.

In order to overcome the difference in height between the functional wings and the main house, there is a segmented stairway leading up to the front loggia. Here it does not serve, as was the case with the Villa Cornaro, as an external symbol of some part of the inner disposition of the villa, but is instead an impressive complement to the main residence as a whole. The harmonious unity of the ensemble is not disturbed by any decoration. Its simple vocabulary of forms fits in smoothly with the villa as a homogenous organism and thereby mediates harmoniously between the practical and public functions of the entire estate.

Right:
Plan
From *I Quattro Libri dell'Architettura*, 1570, volume 2, page 48

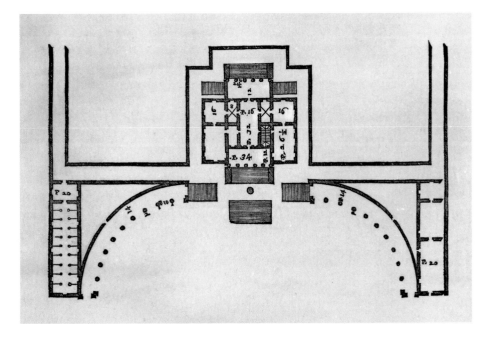

Opposite page:
Façade

1557 ▸ Villa Barbaro
Via Cornuda, Maser, Treviso

Full view

The Villa Barbaro is just as important as an example of a *villa rustica*, i.e. a manor house combined with agricultural activities, as the Villa Rotonda is as an example of a *villa suburbana*, a mansion located just outside of the gates of the city. Its floor plan and execution reflect the social standing of the clients, the brothers Marcantonio and Daniele Barbaro. While Marcantonio played a leading role in the affairs of the Republic of Venice, Daniele was a cleric who had taken part in the Council of Trent as the patriarch of Aquileia.

There is quite a bit of evidence indicating that the Villa Barbaro was built by 1557 or 1558. There could have been no better choice of location: a natural spring became an integral part of this villa ensemble, which was situated halfway up a gently rising hill. A great deal of speculation was connected with this spring, much of it related to the assumption that the site had once been used for cult purposes, and that there may even have been a temple here. Marcantonio Barbaro designed a *nymphaeum* for the spring that was intended to emphasize its symbolic role as a mediator between heavenly and earthly elements and to endow the site with a sort of sacred character.

The façade is marked by admirable harmony. Pavilions at the left and right ends have dovecotes up above and three arches below, in subtle anticipation of the three axes of the main house. Curved buttresses sweep down from the dovecotes to the low *barchessas*, which feature arcades with five arches each. In the middle, the main residence projects forward in a commanding manner. The articulation of its façade is, in contrast to the undecorated buildings to either side, overwhelming. Four colossal half columns connect the ground floor to the *piano nobile* and draw attention up to the projecting interrupted gable, which frames the sculpted crest of the Barbaro family. It suddenly seems to anticipate the High Baroque architecture of an eighteenth century castle—a fascinating vision of the future.

The question as to whether the blending of the sacred and the profane programmes are also reflected by the interior of the villa seems justified. The floor plan of the villa does not provide us with any direct information related to this, even if the main *sala* has a cruciform floor plan. The frescoes play an important role here. In his painting for the Villa Barbaro, Paolo Veronese created a masterpiece. It provides ultimate proof of the builders' intentions to create an idealized artificial world within the real one. In the paintings, motifs from everyday life are combined with others drawn from a sacred context. The Villa Barbaro demonstrates that Paolo Veronese was at the height of his craft as an illusionist painter. One is often tempted to ask: what is illusion, what is fact? Windows framed by columns provide views of an Arcadian landscape, where the idyllic impression is enhanced by ruins from classical antiquity. Close by, one finds real windows that in turn provide views of the real landscape. The interplay that results is extraordinary, and one asks, is the real landscape ennobled by being brought into connection with the ideal landscape, or is the claim to reality on the part of the painted landscape enhanced and manifested by being presented alongside the real landscape?

Nymphaeum with statues of river gods from the workshop of Alessandro Vittoria

However one might be inclined to answer this difficult question, illusionistic painting can be found throughout the interior of the villa. There is a halberd painted in one corner, and a painted hunter steps through an illusionary door as he returns from hunting with his dogs. It is particularly interesting that in the main *sala*, the Olympian hall, the imagery shifts from the profane, on the lower parts of the walls, to the more or less sacred, nearer to the ceiling. Along a balustrade painted all the way around, we see various people depicted in life size and dressed according to style of the day; they seem to be observing what is going on in the villa. The iconographic programme in this large *sala* reaches its pinnacle in the fresco on the vaulted ceiling over this balustrade. This is a depiction of Olympus; the allegory of wisdom at the centre surrounded by Roman gods depicted with their typical symbolic attributes. This wide spectrum of sacred imagery is found on the floor from which the *nymphaeum* with its natural spring is accessed.

Taking all of this into consideration, the Villa Barbaro can indeed be seen as a programmatic building, one that was designed as a means of combining the profane with the sacred. Initially, the profane areas seem to play a greater role, and then the Olympian hall serves as a bridge between the two areas, as if in preparation for the "most holy" site on the estate, the spring. The fact that the Villa Barbaro is virtually built into the side of the hill, makes it seem like an accessory to the spring, one that prepares visitors on the way to it.

Right:
The ceiling frescoes in the main hall are by Paolo Veronese.

Paolo Veronese, portrait of Daniele Barbaro, executed between 1562 and 1570
Galleria Palatina, Palazzo Pitti, Florence

Moreover, this artifice enhances Palladio's efforts to harmoniously combine architecture and landscape to attain a new level of expression that is represented in its ideal form in the Villa Barbaro, one that was never reiterated in villa architecture.

Left page:
View into the cruciform hall in the *piano nobile*

Right:
Detail of the cruciform hall

Plan
From *I Quattro Libri dell'Architettura*, 1570, volume 2, page 51

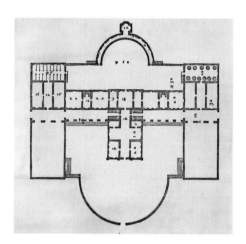

Right:
Sketch of the plan

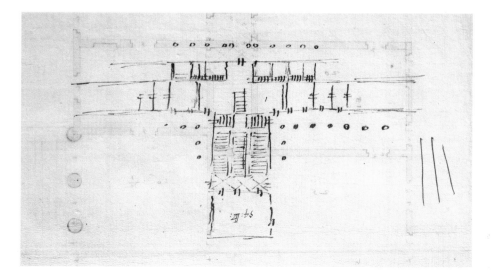

1559 ▸ Villa Foscari
Via dei Turisti, Malcontenta, Venice

Opposite page:
Full view from the south

Full view from the north

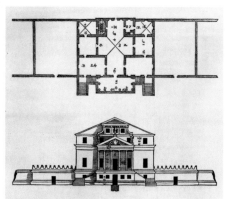

Plan and design for the façade
From *I Quattro Libri dell'Architettura*, 1570, volume 2, page 50

One of Palladio's most beautiful villas can be found on the banks of the Brenta. Its main façade, from which an impressive columned portico projects, is oriented towards the canal. Set on a massive base, it offers visitors who approach the villa from the water, a view of impressive majesty. It is located just outside of the gates of Venice. Originally, it was named after the brothers who had it built, Nicolò and Alvise Foscari, but is, however, better known under the name of the small town where it is located: Malcontenta.

In his design, Palladio broke with tradition by orienting the villa towards the north instead of the south so that it would face the river. The overall appearance is dominated by the portico, which corresponds to the villa in size and is also set on a base. It measures two intercolumniations in depth. The width of the loggia corresponds with that of the entire central *sala*. The façade, which was executed in a somewhat subdued rustication, features moulding in a different colour all the way around the villa to clearly mark the separation between the *piano nobile* and the cellar below and the mezzanine above it. The columns in Ionic order with volutes on either side of the capitals further emphasize this separation. The columns of the portico reach from the base to the moulding marking the ceiling of the *piano nobile*. The loggia figures more prominently here than in the Villa Cornaro in distinguishing between central and subordinate compartments of the building, while at the same time emphasizing the dignified character of the room it represents. The practice of emphasizing the subordinate character of peripheral building compartments by pushing their walls further back is also indicated

Main hall facing south

in the case of the Malcontenta. The extreme projection of the moulding marking the ceiling of the *piano nobile* makes it seem as if the mezzanine level is set further back.

The same principle of subordination, although effected by other means, characterizes the garden façade. Here, again, moulding in a different colour distinguishes the *piano nobile*, and the façade is interrupted—corresponding to the width of the loggia—and merges with the wall surfaces, thereby emphasizing the *sala* on the *piano nobile*. Instead of a triangular gable, as on the main façade, the gable here is open at the bottom to allow the thermal window that it harmoniously frames to rise up into it.

On entering the building through the portal, one gains immediate access to the main hall of the building. The orientation of the main hall on a cruciform floor plan can be seen as a re-adoption of the principle, already applied in the Villa Cornaro, which led to an arrangement of the rooms in a manner that focused all spatial forces on the main hall.

Since the Malcontenta is oriented towards the north, the main hall receives light from the brightest side, namely the south. Palladio made use of this fact. The side across from the entrance has been transformed into a virtual wall of light. A big thermal window echoes the form of the room's vaulting. Under this window, there are another three that fit into an illusionistically painted architecture; the resulting effect

reduces the wall, which is normally experienced as a limitation, to a minimum. This wall of light ensures that the *sala* is virtually flooded with light and thereby further supports the focus of the spatial forces on its centre.

As visitors immediately step into this hall when entering the house, its function is a public one. Hence, it is also richly decorated. In keeping with the ideal of villa culture, the paintings deal with themes of ancient mythology, framed by a painted illusionistic architecture. Here once again we see the blending of interior and exterior structures into a single harmonious whole. The illusionary architecture that is created in the painting is of Ionic order, like the columns of the *piano nobile* on the main façade. The fresco at Malcontenta was done by Giambattista Zeloti and by Battista Franco. Franco died in 1561 leaving his work in the hall of the giants incomplete.

Around 1564 › Villa Emo

Via Stazione, Fanzolo di Vedelago, Treviso

The beginning of construction of the villa is dated at 1555, and the work was presumably completed in 1565: since this is the year in which the marriage of Leonardo di Alvise and Cornelia Grimani is recorded. In the case of the Villa Emo the size of the manor house was expected to correspond with the estate's productivity. And indeed it seems to have been quite productive, since the functional wings of the building are unusually long, a visible sign of prosperity. It also seems safe to assume that the fields that belonged to the villa were highly productive, since the Emos introduced the cultivation of maize on their estate. It was considerably more profitable that the traditional cultivation of millet.

The external appearance of the Villa Emo is characterized by the simple treatment of the entire mass, which is articulated through geometric rhythmization. It represents a purely functional building embodying the idea of the "sacred practice of cultivation", a building that is subordinated to its function and therefore abstains from all ostentation, while still serving as the practical and intellectual centre of the estate. The main residence can at once be recognized because it is raised up above ground level. A wide, open ramp leads up to the loggia; applying temple fronts—a columned portico crowned with a gable—to worldly buildings had by then become a regular part of Palladio's repertoire and served to emphasize the dignity of the villa's owner. As in the case of the Villa Badoer, the loggia does not project from the building as a foyer, but is instead recessed. The emphasis on simplicity even affected the columns used for the loggia, for which Palladio chose the extremely plain Tuscan order.

And yet, the hierarchy of the individual sections of the villa is still expressed. At the ends of the functional wings, recessed dovecotes, called *columbaria*, rise up above the roofs of the functional wings. The impression that they continue on away from the main residence endlessly is interrupted, almost reversed, by these vertical accents. Instead of the dynamic tension being emitted by the main residence and ebbing away on either side; it is discharged by the dovecotes and travels in a subdued form through the agricultural wings to then unfold its full potential in the main residence. The agricultural wings are characterized by the series of arches that visually pave the way for the portico motif and enhance its effect.

The interior of the villa is all the more stately; and the frescoes in the Villa Emo have been preserved in excellent condition to this day. They are attributed to Giambattista Zelotti (1526–1578). Here again we are presented with an abundance of allegorical scenes from ancient mythology, enveloped within highly differentiated illusionistic architecture which was intended to pay tribute to the ideal of *vita in villa*.

Full view with the dovecots to the far left and right

Main hall

Right:
Plan
From *I Quattro Libri dell'Architettura*, 1570,
volume 2, page 55

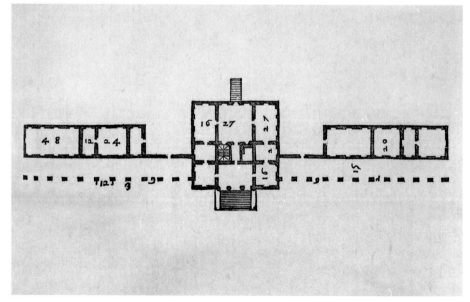

Right:
The fresco shows Hercules and Deianira with the dying centaur—painting attributed to Giambattista Zelotti.

Below:
***Architecture* in the Room of the Arts, fresco by Giambattista Zelotti**
The figure representing Architecture points to the Room of the Arts in the plan of the *piano nobile* of the Villa Emo.

Right:
Drawing of the façade
From *I Quattro Libri dell'Architettura*, 1570, volume 2, page 55

1565 › Chiesa San Giorgio Maggiore
San Giorgio Maggiore, Venice

Right:
San Giorgio Maggiore, seen from the Piazzetta

Below:
Design for the left-hand side of the façade

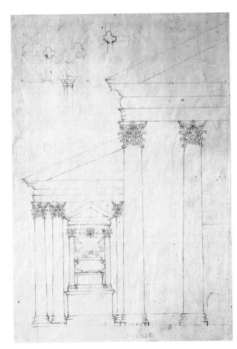

Opposite page:
Main façade

In 982, the Republic of Venice donated the island on the southern side of Saint Mark's Basin to the Benedictines. The monastery grew in economic and ecclesiastical importance in the centuries that followed, making it possible to reconstruct the convent and the church after the Quattrocento. Palladio was commissioned to plan the new church in 1565, after having built the refectory for the monastery between 1560 and 1562. The final step in completing the project was the construction of the façade between 1597 and 1610.

San Giorgio Maggiore takes a prominent place in the panorama of Venice. The church and monastery represent a counterpoint to the buildings on the Piazza San Marco. There was no other architect at that time who seemed as capable of fulfilling the requirements posed by a view along this axis as Palladio, who had already demonstrated his ability to consider perspectives in the landscape in his villas.

At first glance, the façade in front of the middle nave looks like an open temple portico, but then there is a solid wall behind it. The distance between the two middle columns is wider than the intercolumniation on either side; this serves to heighten the "crescendo" effect at the centre. All four columns project three-quarters of the way out of the wall, thereby emphasizing the impression of a free-standing order. In one sketch by Palladio there is in fact a free-standing columned portico.

The first impression upon entering the church is of a longitudinal nave articulated with unusual clarity and great dignity. The three yokes of the nave are separated by colossal columns in Corinthian order set on high pedestals. They support composite capitals, over which a vigorously modelled console cornice projects. Normally, the

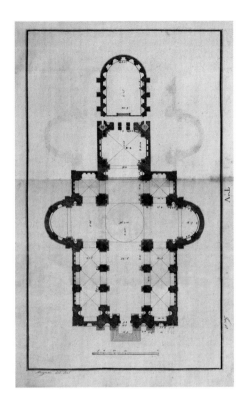

Plan by Ottavio Bertotti Scamozzi
From Ottavio Bertotti Scamozzi, *Le fabbriche
e i disegni di Andrea Palladio*, 1796, volume 4

continuation of the console around corners would have to encompass the vaulting. But this is only partially the case, since above the projecting entablature, the sharp rib ridges between the lunettes begin immediately above the consoles. They form a connection between the round arches of the tripartite thermal windows and the barrel vaulting that encompasses all three yokes, for which decoration was obviously never foreseen.

The rich architectural spectrum of this, Palladio's first, monumental church is far broader than what can be seen from the diverse perspectives along the longitudinal axis. From the crossing, there is a view to the left and the right into the independently articulated transept, which nearly surpasses the long nave in the logical development of its details. From underneath the half domes at both of the semi-circular ends of the transept, there are views of the crossing dome at the other end of the barrel-vaulted rectangular yolk, whose function as a collective centre only completely unfolds when it is seen from this horizontal axis. It conducts the horizontal aspects of the longitudinal nave into a vertical perspective. Since the base of the drum is obscured by the balustrade, the dome appears to be suspended in mid-air.

The importance of San Giorgio Maggiore in terms of the history of European architecture can only be compared with that of Michelangelo's design for Saint Peter's in Rome. Palladio articulated the volume of the building, in its entirety and its individual parts, to a degree never before seen. The sculptural elements do not simply seem to have been fitted onto the walls, but instead, to have developed out of them. By enabling the enclosure around a space to actively set force in motion, Palladio established one of the preconditions for European Baroque. In addition, Palladio overturned the practice of simply combining individual parts by striving to create a unified space, and although he was unable to fully realize this goal, it is still recognizable as such. Most importantly, Palladio developed each of the individual elements from a single idea common to all parts: this was of virtually revolutionary importance, especially in a Venetian context. Finally, an essential step was taken towards the integration of the long nave into the central plan church, a problem that was destined to be of great concern to architects in the seventeenth century.

1565‣Palazzo Valmarana
Corso Fogazzaro, Vicenza

Sketches of the street and courtyard façades for the plate in: *I Quattro Libri dell'Architettura*, 1570

The dominance of supporting forces is primarily exhibited in the façade of the Palazzo Valmarana by its six colossal pilasters. They extend over both storeys and support an attic, which projects forward considerably and upon which the mezzanine level rests. These pilasters stand on a continuous base that projects further forward directly below the pilasters, thereby forming pedestals at ground level which are, in turn, framed by rusticated blocks. In the vertical articulation of the façade, the pilasters are the most prominent design feature. Behind them the surfaces of the walls are staggered in a highly differentiated manner. By choosing the colossal pilaster instead of columns in colossal order, as proposed in an earlier plan, the Palazzo Valmarana is able to take a prominent position on the street, and still be integrated into the existing row of buildings. Instead of the rhythmic swelling of columns of colossal order, we encounter the static tranquillity of pilasters, which correspond with the strict vertical articulation of the adjacent buildings. How important it was to Palladio to integrate the Palazzo Valmarana into the existing row of buildings is demonstrated by the two outer yokes of the façade. The colossal order of the pilasters is abandoned here. Instead, the pilasters on the corners are only the height of the *pianterreno* and are replaced in the *piano nobile* by sculptures of warriors that support the projecting attic cornice. The colossal order

Façade facing Corso Fogazzaro

of the Palazzo Valmarana is thereby organically adapted to the two-storey façades of the adjacent buildings.

The altered articulation of the storeys is reflected in the fenestration of the two external segments of the façade. Both in the *pianterreno* and in the *piano nobile* the windows are smaller than in the remaining façade. The vertical tendency of the palace façade is limited in these façade segments in two ways: instead of the entablatures featuring reliefs above the four inner windows of the rusticated *pianterreno*, there are mezzanine windows that attract considerable shadows on the far left and far right, and which are separated from the regular windows by a narrow staggered cornice. The windows in the external yokes of the *piano nobile* are the only ones with triangular gables up above them. While here the strict colossal articulation of the façade is counteracted by elements that generate shadows, the remainder of the façade between these segments is completely subordinated to the dominance of the colossal pilasters.

1565▸Palazzo Schio
Façade ▸ Contrà San Marco, Vicenza

The main façade, which was designed by Palladio in 1565/66, was relatively narrow and encompassed only three axes. Although the façade of the *piano nobile* was segmented in a rigidly geometric manner, there is still a pronounced tendency to avoid unarticulated surfaces. In conforming to this, Palladio divided the wall into a number of layers of different depths. First of all, there are four three-quarter columns with Corinthian style capitals installed in front with bases that are integrated into the rustication of the socle. There are three windows in the intercolumniations with sills resting on the socle. In order to ensure that the windows appear to be properly integrated into the masonry, there are balusters in front of the windows. Triangular gables that project far out of the wall fill in much of the area between the windows and the architrave. The moulding around the windows also projects considerably, thereby casting shadows. The light that falls onto the façade of the palace thus becomes a decisive element in its design, because the remaining wall surfaces are modulated by the shadows that fall on them. The mezzanine windows, once featured in the façade, are likely to have enhanced this effect. Palladio delivered them from their more or less subordinate role in the façade by allowing them to reach beyond their own storey and penetrate the architrave.

1566·Villa Almerico ("La Rotonda")
Via della Rotonda, Vicenza

Façade from the northwest

Between 1566 and 1570 Count Paolo Almerico, an advisor to Popes Pius IV and Pius V, had a house erected, a *villa suburbana*—i.e. a country house not for agriculture, but only for residential and leisure purposes—that passed into the ownership of Count Capra in 1591 (hence the inscription on the plaque over the main entrance). The attic was not built until 1725–1740, although it was obviously planned by Palladio, since it is depicted in his *Quattro libri dell'Architettura*, and was an essential component of his intentions. Because of the completely symmetrical arrangement of its design around a circular centre the building was soon referred to as "La Rotonda".

The building is characterized by perfectly symmetrical proportions. In the tradition of classical antiquity, its beauty is derived from the harmony of the numbers and proportion, or to quote Vitruvius: the proper agreement between the members of the work itself, and relation between the different parts. Gabled porticoes with five columns are found on all four sides of the central core. Hence, there is no differentiation between the main façade and the secondary ones, and the socle is the same height as the attic. The porticoes take up half of the overall width. The portico and stairs each correspond to half of the diameter of the core building. This is, in turn, identical to the overall height, so that the core of the building looks like a cube from outside.

The concept of a central plan, which was realized here to such perfection, seems like a "purely" artificial structure in comparison to the natural world around it.

In his *Quattro libri* Palladio explains: "The site is as pleasant and delightful as can be found; because it is upon a small hill, of very easy access ... it is encompassed by the

Opposite page:
Full view from the east

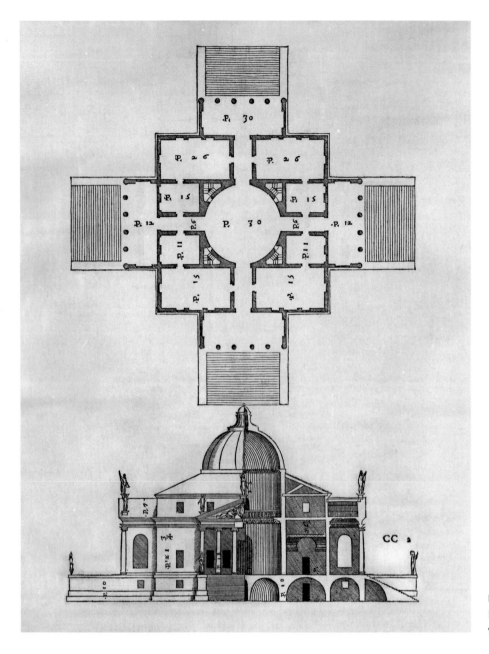

Plan and cross-section
From *I Quattro Libri dell' Architettura*, 1570,
volume 2, page 19

most pleasant risings, which look like a very great theatre ... and therefore, as it enjoys the most beautiful views from all sides ... there are loggias on all the four fronts." Guided by Palladio in this manner, we are able to approach this building in an entirely different manner; it seems to grow up out of the landscape, the stairways on the façades echo the incline of the terrain, the central dome can be seen as an amplification of the hilltop. Does the central plan building crown the site—or, conversely, does the hill grow up through the building? Organic growth—nature—and the abstract—precisely calculated architectural form—penetrate each other.

Anyone entering the villa expecting to find all lines of sight unified at the centre of the domed hall—a spot clearly marked by a circle of coloured marble on the floor—will undoubtedly be surprised by the darkness of this windowless room. One's gaze is drawn through the narrow access ways connecting the porticoes to the domed hall on all four sides to the sun-drenched landscape outside. Centring and centrifugal forces

View through one of the accesses to the central hall

generate tension in a diametrical relationship to each other. This contrast can be recognized as a design element that became characteristic of Mannerism.

Unfortunately, there is no information on Palladio's ideas for the interior design of the main room. The painting found there today was not done until 1680–1687 by Lodovico Dorigny and his assistants. Its effect is an irrational "destruction" of the walls and their architectural structure.

The Villa Rotonda gave rise to a vast tradition in villa architecture. It was a formative building in the history of European architecture and was already copied in 1576, by Vincenzo Scamozzi in the Rocca Pisana in Lonigo. Neo-Palladianism also played a central role in profane architecture during the Baroque period in England, as seen in the example of Mereworth Castle (Kent) built by Colin Campbell between 1722 and 1726.

Central hall
The subjects of the frescoes on the lower part of
the walls are drawn from classical mythology.

Dome of the central hall

1569 · Villa Sarego
Via Ca' Dedè, Pedemonte di Valpolicella, Verona

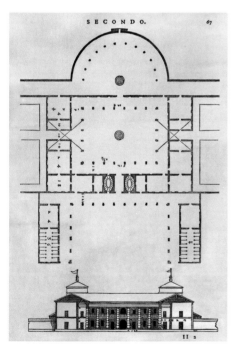

Plan and elevation
From *I Quattro Libri dell'Architettura*, 1570, volume 2, page 67

Within the context of Palladio's oeuvre, the designs he drew for this impressive ensemble, around 1570, are quite unusual. The exact role of the client's desire to see his ambition to power reflected in the architecture will never be known. There is, however, no overlooking the fact that if the entire, massive ensemble had ever been completed, it would not have blended in with the surrounding landscape to form a single entity, its fortress-like appearance would, in fact, have prohibited any convergence. The assumption that Palladio intended to make a reference in his design to the military tradition of this Veronese family, the Saregos, may be an explanation for the unusual approach taken by the architect.

The only part of this larger ensemble to ever be built was the left half of the main residence and the loggia that belonged to it. In this courtyard, Palladio seems to have blended two elements drawn from Vitruvius' texts and Leone Battista Alberti's reconstructed Roman residence, namely the atrium and the peristyle. Whether a courtyard designed with a two-storey colonnade surrounding it can be considered successful, is subject to doubt. Just try to imagine the effect of this courtyard if it had been completed. The massive colossal pillars would have unleashed forces that would not have had enough space to unfold within the courtyard. On the one hand, this might be seen as the clever blending of an atrium and a columned courtyard; however, on the other hand, this sophistication is counteracted by the visual impression that the elements used in designing the courtyard are exaggerated and, thereby, more closely aligned with Mannerist architecture.

1571 ▸ Loggia del Capitaniato
Piazza dei Signori, Vicenza

Opposite page:

View of the main façade from the basilica opposite it

The Loggia del Capitaniato, located on the Piazza dei Signori across from the main façade of the Basilica, is the most impressive example of a building designed to represent urban authority from Palladio's late period. Four colossal three-quarter columns rise up from pedestals carved out of white stone. Their dynamic rise is continued in the tall composite capitals which are derived from a combination of the Corinthian and Ionic orders. The vertical movement is echoed by the returning of the cornices and the continuous balustrade and comes to an end in the flat pilasters of the final half storey. Despite the importance of the variation in colour between white stone and red brick for the overall effect, the building by no means seems to be composed mainly of small pieces of brick. As in many of Palladio's other works, the monumentality of the forms that he rendered triumphs over the material. The stark relief of the main façade, which results from the apparent emergence of the columns from the wall, is enhanced by the way the balconies project far beyond the windows of the *piano nobile* and by the vigorously expansive balustrade cornice. Light and shadow combine in the duet of coloured material. In comparison, the architectural structure is not obscured by the lavish stucco decoration on the remaining wall surfaces. It is presumably from the workshop of Lorenzo Rubini, who is often mentioned in connection with Palladio's works, and creates the impression of having been added after the fact, and not of an essential element of the building.

The original seat of Venetian military authority in Vicenza, built on this site at the beginning of the fifteenth century, had been marked by a large columned hall, which was described as damaged on 18 April 1571. The construction of the new building was apparently begun shortly thereafter. There is no doubting Palladio's authorship since his name is inscribed on the façade under the balcony on the left: *Andrea Palladio i(nventore) archit(ecto)*.

There is good reason to believe that the original project allowed for five or even seven axes. The assumption that originally the façade should have been extended to five axes seems justified because two additional columns to the left would have brought the building precisely into line with the Basilica.

For modern day visitors, however, the Loggia del Capitaniato seems very cohesive. While in the Basilica the impression of layers predominates, vertical extension is the overriding theme in the Loggia del Capitaniato. Moreover, in his late work Palladio confronted the equality of the individual parts, alongside and with each other, with the dominance of a single motif to which the others, in a rich orchestration of elements, subordinate themselves in order to act as supporting voices. Not least of all, the—albeit many times layered—"relief" found on the loggia of the Basilica gives way here to a virtually baroque power of modulation.

While the stark fragmentation of the surfaces and their envelopment in decorative elements may also seem "manneristic", the overall impression provided a perspective for the future. The door to the Baroque age was now open.

1576 · Chiesa del Redentore
La Giudecca, Venice

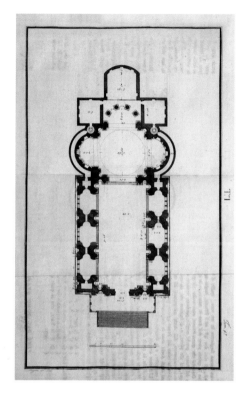

Plan by Ottavio Bertotti Scamozzi
From Ottavio Bertotti Scamozzi, *Le fabbriche e i disegni di Andrea Palladio*, 1796, volume 4

Opposite page:
Full view from the Canale della Giudecca

On 4 September 1576 the Venetian Senate decided to fund a votive church dedicated to the Redeemer in order to rid the city of a serious epidemic of the plague. A prominent location within the city was to be sought. A committee, which was quickly formed, recommended a site directly on the Giudecca, across from the Piazzetta di San Marco, in direct proximity to the Capuchin monastery that would subsequently assume responsibility for the church.

On 23 November 1576, Palladio was commissioned to build the church. He was asked to submit two designs, one for a long form and another with a "round" floor plan. Marcantonio Barbaro, an old friend and patron of Palladio's, favoured the project with the "round" floor plan. However, on 9 January 1577, the majority of the committee members ultimately decided in favour of the longitudinal church, not least of all because of the influence of the decrees of the Council of Trent.

The long nave was better suited to the functions for which the building was to be used: processions, votive rituals and as a monastery church. Another important factor was undoubtedly the Counter-Reformation's aversion to the central plan church, which was seen as a heathen form, since it was borrowed from antiquity.

On 27 September 1592 the consecration of the church was celebrated. Since 1593 there has been an annual procession on the third Sunday in July from the Palace of the Doge across the Canale Grande and, with the help of a temporary bridge, from the Zattere, the street along the shore of the main island across from the Giudecca, to the new church. In terms of urban planning, Palladio was confronted with a task similar to San Giorgio Maggiore. The façade of the new church, which would be turned slightly towards the façade of San Giorgio, had to establish a connection across the water to the buildings on the Piazzetta San Marco. For the sake of a visual connection, Palladio used some of the basic motifs from his earlier work again, but formed them into something entirely new. The sections on the side with the outer edges of raked gables and a "temple portico" with a colossal order and dominating middle gable do not appear to be standing free before the front wall of the long nave, since they are backed by solid walls. Set back, they form a second storey, enclosed on the sides by the raked gables, which are interrupted in the middle by a horizontal console cornice, over which a hipped roof echoes the angle of the gables and leads further towards the dome between the two slender bell turrets. Hence, the façade forms the front of a cube that is composed of individual layers. It is not a case of the "temple front" with a wall erected behind the columns serving as a façade, but rather a pre-existing wall that was modelled with the motifs of a temple front.

Since the low height of the buildings on either side of the Redentore makes it visible at a great distance, Palladio took great care in designing the flanks. On the lower level, the brick masonry is articulated by double pilasters with Corinthian capitals, between which there are niches in the lower part of the wall—in anticipation of the design of the walls inside. In the clerestory, double traverse arches form an optical extension of the pilasters. However, the relationship between the individual elements only serves to

emphasize the fundamentally different nature of the concept of this space. First of all, the Redentore is not a three-nave basilica, but a longitudinal nave augmented by side chapels. Then these chapels do not open up to the middle in regular succession, but instead in the form of a *rhythmic travée*, i.e. wall sections with wide openings followed by narrower closed sections. Two systems of threes penetrate each other: alternatively, the engaged colossal columns can be seen as part of the closed wall surfaces or the chapel openings.

Communication and penetration are also characteristic of the other elements used for articulation. Instead of the high pedestals for the colossal half columns found in the longitudinal nave of San Giorgio Maggiore, Palladio uses low rectangular socles so that the chapels and the central space are more closely connected. By including two niches, one above the other, in the closed, narrow fields, the wall seems to recede, an allusion is made to the chapel opening, and these niches are visually related to the

Cross-section by Ottavio Bertotti Scamozzi
From Ottavio Bertotti Scamozzi, *Le fabbriche e i disegni di Andrea Palladio*, 1796, volume 4

niches in the horizontal walls between the chapels. The interplay between expansive elements installed in front of the walls, niches and chapel openings make the walls seem highly animated in relief—almost like a premonition of Baroque solutions in which the encompassing walls undulate back and forth.

What had fundamentally changed since San Giorgio Maggiore was the relationship between the wall and the vaulting. While Palladio established the connection between the monumental cornice and the chapel openings by using volutes, he continued the cornice—expanded to an architrave by extensive moulding—around the main nave without any returns. There is no direct connection to the vaulting. In fact, because its springing point is obscured by the architrave, which projects far from the wall, it seems to float over the nave—as if developed from the solution adopted for the dome of San Giorgio Maggiore and a preliminary study for the vaulting of the Tempietto in Maser. Consequently, the vaulting attains a unity that was barely imaginable in San Giorgio. In-

Elevation by Ottavio Bertotti Scamozzi
From Ottavio Bertotti Scamozzi, *Le fabbriche e i disegni di Andrea Palladio*, 1796, volume 4

Opposite page:
View from the south

stead of the sharp triangular lunettes that begin just above the point where the cornice surrounds the columns, here we find spherical arches of the intersecting vaults—again adapted to the forms used throughout.

The impression for visitors stepping into the crossing is of a harmonious central plan church with its own order and an elongated western arm. There may still be some reverberation from the impressions Palladio gathered while studying Michelangelo's choir solution for Saint Peter's in Rome. No other solution to the problem of combining a longitudinal nave and a central plan church in the sixteenth century was more successful. In the Redentore Andrea Palladio realized a building that easily fulfils the three requirements placed on it: it has a longitudinal nave for the procession, a triconchos for the votive ritual and an adjacent monk's choir for the liturgical functions for the Capuchins responsible for caring for the church. The question as to whether the Redentore was based on an additional iconological programme in the sense of *architecture parlante* ("speaking architecture" in which a building explains itself) must be approached cautiously: notable are the repetitions of tri-partite elements in the floor plan and elevation. In keeping with the Redentore's function, it consists of three very different spaces located one after the other, but which are still very closely connected, and the number three is characteristic of the articulation of the longitudinal nave as well as the form of the presbytery. Was this intended as an allusion to the Holy Trinity in addition to the Redeemer's patronage of the church? There is no evidence to this effect in the documents that have been preserved.

Despite some great stylistic differences, the standard according to which Palladio's Redentore must be measured, in terms of historical development, is Leone Battista Alberti's pioneering 1470 design for the Church of San Andrea in Mantua. It provided Palladio with an example of a nave spanned by uniform barrel vaulting, the system of a *rhythmic travée* with barrel vaulted side chapels and recessed narrow wall areas, as well as a dominant domed crossing. But a comparison shows Palladio's specific contribution: the whole not seen as a sum of its individual parts, but instead the parts as necessary segments of the whole; the enclosing walls seen not as the harmony of properly articulated surfaces, but as the embodiment of sculpturally modelled segments that affect the impression of "interim space", the importance of spatial orientation seen not in the careful balance between the horizontal and the vertical, but as a factor in the carefully calculated upward thrust. Here again the only standards in the history of architecture in the sixteenth century suitable for comparison are those set by Michelangelo.

1580 ▸ Tempietto Barbaro
Strada Comunale Bassanese, Maser, Treviso

Cross-section by Ottavio Bertotti Scamozzi
From Ottavio Bertotti Scamozzi, *Le fabbriche e i disegni di Andrea Palladio*, 1796, volume 4

At the end of his life, Palladio finally had the opportunity to build a central plan church: the Tempietto Barbaro in Maser. The combination "temple front" and domed building includes references to the Pantheon in Rome, on which it was modelled. In actual fact, two forms of central plan architecture intersect in its floor plan: the circle and the Greek cross. The exterior is oriented completely to the façade. An unusually steep portico, set far forward of the building mass, leads with its raked gables up to the two small bell towers, which in turn help to further communicate the upward sweep of the dome. The five intercolumniations are framed by pillars.

Inside there are niches of alternating depths between eight uniform embedded half columns in a rectangular floor plan and closed wall segments with tabernacles to display figures. A continuous cornice, with moulding that consisted of three flat bands separated from each other by egg and dart enrichment carried over from the arcade arches, completes the substructure. A permeated balustrade forms the transition to the dome vaulting. The base of the dome, which is shifted slightly outwards, is not visible: in continuation of the solution designed for the crossing dome of San Giorgio Maggiore, it seems to float in space—an incunabula of similar solutions from the Late Baroque period.

Although it is very reminiscent of the Pantheon in Rome, because of its general disposition, a closer comparison illustrates the differences: in the ancient building the vertical masonry and vaulting appear to be part of a uniform, solid encasement. In this late work, Palladio clearly distinguishes between the cylinder and the hemisphere by repeatedly emphasizing the horizontal. He also separates a plastically tangible earthly

The interior

zone from the light-flooded heavenly zone that cannot be precisely fathomed by just looking at it.

The overabundant stucco decorations created by craftsmen associated with the sculptor Alessandro Vittoria can hardly have been intended by Palladio. With regard to the final appearance of the interior, one might justifiably claim that: "This irreverent child of the Pantheon is more Rococo than Roman" (James S. Ackerman).

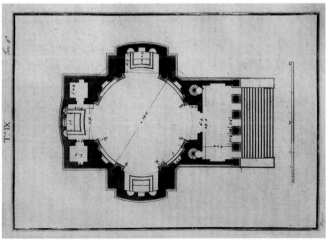

View of the Tempietto from the Villa Barbaro

Left:
Plan by Ottavio Bertotti Scamozzi
From Ottavio Bertotti Scamozzi, *Le fabbriche e i disegni di Andrea Palladio*, 1796, volume 4

1580 · Teatro Olimpico
Piazza Matteotti, Vicenza

Opposite page:
View of the proscenium from the upper loggia

View of the proscenium

Since the founding of the Olympic Academy in Vicenza, of which Palladio was a charter member, theatre productions had been staged at the relatively unsatisfactory *Casa Accademica*. On 15 February 1580, the decision was taken to build a theatre. Palladio was asked to submit proposals and a model, and construction was already begun on 20 February 1580. His ability to submit the design at such short notice was a result of the fact that he had been pondering the problems involved in designing a theatre for nearly two decades. He planned a richly articulated proscenium made of wood and rising up over three storeys, each different from the other. The motif of the lower floor is one of an extended triumphal arch. Free-standing columns in front of pilasters form three axes on either side of the central archway. The middle of these three axes is open as a rectangular doorway. The outer ones feature tabernacle niches framed by smaller columns and triangular gables. A broad free-standing arch resting on columns forms the centre of this *scenae frons* that reaches well up into the middle storey. This is, in turn, not as tall and is also more restrained in terms of its sculptural modulation. The cornice above this middle storey principally repeats the mouldings of the cornice marking the wallhead of the lower stories, but—in keeping with the reduced height of the walls—it is also less pronounced. This is topped off by a stylized attic, which is further reduced both in height and sculptural modulation; its individual axes are separated by pilasters only.

Hence, from the bottom to the top there is a "diminuendo" in the scale and in the modulation of the wall. Considering Palladio's earlier work, it comes as no surprise that all of the rich variations of the individual details are not only related to each other

Full view of the interior

Right:
Plan by Ottavio Bertotti Scamozzi
From Ottavio Bertotti Scamozzi, *Le fabbriche e i
disegni di Andrea Palladio*, 1786, volume 1

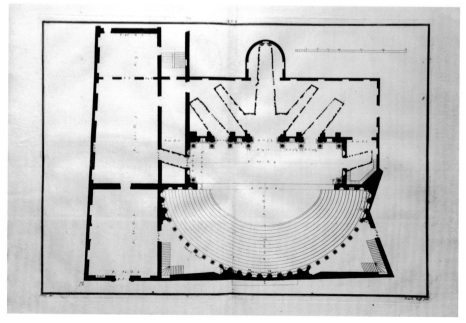

but also connected with each other. However, Palladio had never before included horizontal and vertical values in such a differentiated and dense network of elements that interpenetrated each other.

The front of the stage and the seating area stand in vibrant contradiction to each other. The stairs of the auditorium rise up from the semicircle of the *orchestra*. At the back it is delineated by a Corinthian order colonnade with some open and some closed intercolumniations. All along the semi-circular perforated balustrade at the top of the back wall there is another series of stucco figures, which were conceived as a transition to the open sky. As a consequence, we are confronted with the question as to how the auditorium was to be enclosed at the top according to the original plan. The current solution, a flat ceiling with a blue sky and scattered clouds, dates from 1914. It may very well be similar to the sixteenth century plans, since they undoubtedly foresaw the illusion of a space that was open at the top.

Palladio did not live to see the completion of the Teatro Olimpico. On 6 May 1584 a contract was signed with Vincenzo Scamozzi, who made a series of changes to the original project. He had side walls built between the auditorium and the proscenium, thus creating an enclosed stage. Not only did Scamozzi create a division in what Palladio presumably intended to be a unified proscenium and seating area (*cavea*), he also made lasting changes to the overall effect of the stage façade. He artfully created views of the street through the entrances to the *scenae frons* that were perspectively foreshortened. Through an incline in the level of the floor and the gradual narrowing of the streets he was able to open up the stage wall, which was closed despite its rich articulation.

In 1584 the theatre was inaugurated with a performance of the tragedy *Oedipus Rex* by Sophocles.

Cross-section by Ottavio Bertotti Scamozzi
From Ottavio Bertotti Scamozzi, *Le fabbriche e i disegni di Andrea Palladio*, 1786, volume 1

Life and Work

1508 ▶ Palladio is born as Andrea di Pietro, the son of a miller in Padua, on 8 November 1508.

1521 ▶ Palladio's father signs a six-year apprenticeship contract for his son in the workshop of the architect and stone carver Bartolomeo Cavazza da Sossano in Padua.

1523 ▶ Palladio flees from Cavazza's workshop to Vicenza, but is forced to return in order to fulfil his contract.

1524 ▶ Palladio becomes a member of the Masons' and Stone Carvers' Guild in Vicenza and is taken on in the respected workshop of Giovanni di Giacomo da Porlezza in Pedemuro.

1530 ▶ His attempt to establish a workshop of his own fails.

1534 ▶ Marries Allegradonna, the daughter of a cabinetmaker. The marriage produces four sons and one daughter.

1537–1542
Villa Godi, Lugo di Vicenza

1538 ▶ In February his first encounter with Count Giangiorgio Trissino, who introduces Palladio to a refined circle of potential clients in Vicenza.

around 1539/40
Villa Piovene, Lugo di Vicenza (central block without a foyer)

1540 ▶ Palladio is awarded the professional title of architect on 26 August.

after 1540
Villa Gazzotti, Bertesina
Casa Cilena, Vicenza

1541 ▶ In summer, his first journey to Rome with Count Trissino.

1541–1542
Villa Forni-Cerato, Montecchio

1542
Villa Pisani, Bagnolo

after 1542
Palazzo Thiene, Vicenza

1545
Villa Thiene, Quinto
Villa Saraceno, Finale

1545/46 ▶ Second journey to Rome in the company of Trissino. Trissino bestows the name Palladio upon Andrea di Pietro after Pallas Athene, the goddess of the arts.

1546/47 ▶ During another stay in Rome, Palladio also devotes himself to studies in Tivoli, Palestrina and Albano.

1548/49
Villa Caldogno, Caldogno

1549 ▶ His hopes of attaining a position in the building lodge of Saint Peter in Rome are dashed by the death of Pope Paul III. On 11 April Palladio is called upon to become the chief architect of the Palazzo della Ragione in Vicenza.
Palazzo della Ragione ("Basilica"), Vicenza (designation as chief architect)

before 1550
Palazzo Iseppo Porto, Vicenza
Villa Poiana, Poiana Maggiore

1550
Palazzo Chiericati, Vicenza

1552 ▶ Invitation by Cardinal Christoforo Madruzzi to Trento; stay in Innsbruck.

1552–1555
Villa Pisani, Montagnana

1553
Villa Cornaro, Piombino Dese

1554 ▶ Palladio completes his book *L'Antichità di Roma*.

Glossary

around 1555
Villa Chiericati, Vancimuglio

1556 ▶ Founding member of the "Olympic Academy" in Vicenza.

1556
Palazzo Antonini, Udine
Arco Bollani, Udine

after 1556
Villa Badoer, Fratta Polesine

1557/58
Palazzo Comunale, Feltre
Villa Barbaro, Maser

1559/60
Villa Foscari, Malcontenta

1560/61
Santa Maria della Carità, Venice, cloisters

1560–1562
San Giorgio Maggiore, Venice, refectory

after 1562
San Francesco della Vigna, Venice, façade

1563/64
Villa Valmarana, Lisiera

around 1564
Villa Emo, Fanzolo

before 1565
Pretorio, Cividale

1565
San Giorgio Maggiore, Venice, church
Cathedral, Vicenza, apse, vault
Palazzo Valmarana, Vicenza

before 1566
Palazzo Schio, Vicenza, façade
Villa Zeno, Cessalto

1566 ▶ Guest of Count Emanuele Filiberto of Savoy in Turin. From there, Palladio travels to Provence. The Accademia del Disegno in Florence inducts him as a member.

1566–1570
Villa Almerico ("La Rotonda"), Vicenza

1568 ▶ Palladio declines an invitation to the Imperial Court in Vienna because he is overburdened with work.

around 1568/69
Villa Sarego, Pedemonte di Valpolicella

1570 ▶ Palladio becomes Sansovino's successor as the advising architect to the Republic of Venice. Publication of *I Quattro libri dell'Architettura.*

1570/71
Palazzo Barbarano, Vicenza

1570–1580
Palazzo Porto-Breganze, Vicenza

1571
Loggia del Capitaniato, Vicenza

1576
Santa Corona, Vicenza
Valmarana Chapel, Vicenza

1576/77
Chiesa del Redentore, Venice

around 1579/80
Le Zitelle, Venice (changed)

1579
Porta Gemona, San Daniele del Friuli

1579/80
Tempietto Barbaro, Maser
Teatro Olimpico, Vicenza

1580 ▶ On 19 August Palladio dies in Vicenza or Maser.

Attic ▶ Low storey above the main cornice of a building, usually completed by a cornice at the top
Barchessas ▶ Roofed passageways
Clerestory ▶ The upper part of the nave, transepts and choir of a basilica, containing windows. The height of the celestory exceeds that of the aisles adjacent to the main nave
Columbaria ▶ Here: dovecot, usually used in the figurative sense to designate a repository for urns
Corbel ▶ A block, usually of stone, projecting from a wall
Crossing ▶ Space where the nave intersects the transept in a church with a quadratic floor plan
Intercolumniation ▶ The area between two columns, measured in the diameters of the columns
Loggia ▶ A gallery or an open passageway integrated into the façade of a building
Metope ▶ Square, decorated space between two triglyphs in the frieze of the Doric order
Mezzanine ▶ Low storey, (between two higher ones) in which servants' quarters or functional rooms were located
Nymphaeum ▶ Fountain dedicated to a nymph
Peristyle ▶ Courtyard surrounded by a colonnade
Piano nobile ▶ Main storey of a building
Pilaster ▶ A rectangular column projecting from the wall with base and capital
Portico ▶ A porch with a loggia
Risalit ▶ A part of a building projecting from the façade over the full height of the building
Rustication ▶ Façade construction in rough-hewn blocks
Sala ▶ The large hall in the *piano nobile*
Scenae frons ▶ Architecturally structured wall behind the stage
Serliana ▶ Archway flanked by two rectangular openings. Antique motif often used by Serlio and further developed by Palladio, therefore also called the Palladian motif
Triglyphes ▶ Relief fields in the Doric order articulated by grooves

Italy

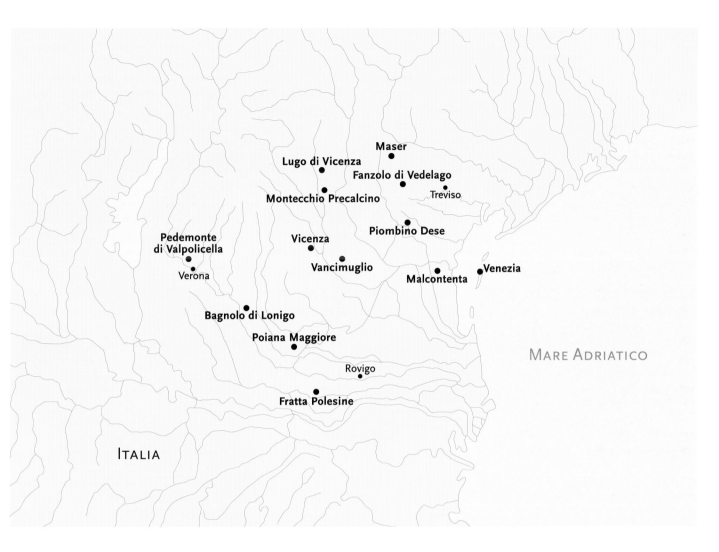

Bagnolo di Lonigo, Vicenza
Villa Pisani

Fanzolo di Vedelago, Treviso
Villa Emo

Fratta Polesine, Rovigo
Villa Badoer

Lugo di Vicenza
Villa Godi
Villa Piovene

Malcontenta, Venice
Villa Foscari

Maser, Treviso
Tempietto Barbaro
Villa Barbaro

Montecchio Precalcino, Vicenza
Villa Forni-Cerato

Pedemonte di Valpolicella, Verona
Villa Sarego

Piombino Dese, Padua
Villa Cornaro

Poiana Maggiore, Vicenza
Villa Poiana

Vancimuglio, Vicenza
Villa Chiericati

Venice
Chiesa del Redentore
Chiesa San Giorgio Maggiore

Vicenza
Loggia del Capitaniato
Palazzo Chiericati
Palazzo della Ragione ("Basilica")
Palazzo Schio
Palazzo Valmarana
Teatro Olimpico
Villa Almerico ("La Rotonda")

Bibliography

Credits

▶ Ackerman, James S. *Palladio*. Baltimore/ Hamondsworth, 1966.

▶ Bertotti-Scamozzi, Ottavio. *Le fabbriche e i disegni di Andrea Palladio*. Vol. 1–4. Vicenza, 1776–1783.

▶ Bertotti Scamozzi, Ottavio. *Les bâtiments et les desseins de André Palladio*. Vol. 4. Vicenza, 1796.

▶ Beyer, Andreas. *Andrea Palladio. Das Teatro Olimpico*. Frankfurt am Main, 1987.

▶ Boucher, Bruce. *Andrea Palladio. The Architect in his Time*. New York/London, 2nd ed, 2007.

▶ Constant, Caroline. *The Palladio Guide*. Princeton, 1985.

▶ Forssmann, Erik. *Palladios Lehrgebäude*. Uppsala, 1965.

▶ Goethe, Johann Wolfgang von. *Die italienische Reise*. Munich, 1960.

▶ Muraro, Michelangelo. *The Venetian Villas*. Udine, 1986.

▶ Muttoni, Francesco. *Architettura di Andrea Palladio Vicentino con le osservazioni dell'Architetto N.N.* 9 Vol. Venice, 1740–1748.

▶ Palladio, Andrea. *The Four Books of Architecture*. Reprint of the 1738 translation, by Isaac Ware, of *I Quattro libri dell'Architettura*, Venice 1570. Mineola (N.Y.), 1965.

▶ Pée, Herbert. *Die Palastbauten des Andrea Palladio*. Würzburg, 1941.

▶ Puppi, Lionello. *Andrea Palladio. Das Gesamtwerk*. 2 Vol. Stuttgart, 1977.

▶ Puppi, Lionello. *Palladio Drawings*. New York, 1990.

▶ Spielmann, Heinz. *Andrea Palladio und die Antike*. Munich, 1966.

▶ Vitruvius. *The Ten Books on Architecture*, translated by Morris Hicky Morgan. Mineola (N.Y.), 1960.

▶ Wundram, Manfred and Pape, Thomas. *Andrea Palladio 1508–1580. Architekt zwischen Renaissance und Barock*. Cologne, 1988.

▶ Zorzi, Alvise. *Rupubblica del leone: storia di Venezia*. Milan, 1979.